Growing in Christ

Laying the Foundations for Christian Maturity

This book belongs to

_____

GARY E. GILLEY

Growing in Christ

Laying the Foundations for Christian Maturity

Gary E. Gilley

LARKSPUR, COLORADO

Grace Acres Press
PO Box 22
Larkspur, CO 80118
www.GraceAcresPress.com

Printed in United States of America
25 24 23 22 21 20 19   01 02 03 04 05 06 07 08

Print ISBN: 978-1-60265-064-0
Ebook ISBN: 978-1-60265-065-7

Grace Acres Press also publishes books in a variety of electronic formats. Some content that appears in print may not be available in electronic books.

Library of Congress Control Number: 2019953193

Contents

Introduction

As we search the New Testament (NT) Scriptures for instruction concerning spiritual growth and maturity, we find that Philippians 2:12–13 pulls many threads together and offers a perfect summary. It reads: *So then, my beloved, just as you have always obeyed, not as in my presence only, but now much more in my absence, work out your salvation with fear and trembling; for it is God who is at work in you, both to will and to work for His good pleasure.*

From this text, we learn that the Christian life is very much a two-sided coin. While salvation is wholly a work of the Lord, requiring only faith and not our personal efforts, such is not true of sanctification, or spiritual growth. Rather, both God and the believer play vital, sometimes overlapping roles, in our progress toward maturity. Side-by-side, without any apology whatsoever, God tells us that we must work out our own salvation, but also that He is at work in our lives to accomplish His purposes. What does this look like?

The words "work out" are the translation of a Greek word which means to carry out toward a goal, or to carry to its ultimate conclusion. If a teacher tells students to work out a math problem, the teacher means to carry it to its ultimate conclusion, to the end result. That is the idea behind the wording here. The Philippians, to whom Paul was writing, and all believers by application, are exhorted to carry their salvation to its ultimate conclusion: namely, to become more like Christ. That is, Paul is commanding them (and this is a command) to produce Christlikeness in their own lives. The tense of the verb indicates that Paul is expecting continuous, sustained, strenuous exertion. This is a lifetime project, and we must aim at nothing less than spiritual perfection. Paul, in the next chapter, admits that he himself has never achieved this perfection, but it is his goal and he is making great efforts to obtain it (3:12–14).

In verse 13, a great truth of Scripture is revealed when the inspired apostle writes, *For it is God who is at work in you, both to will and to work for His good pleasure.* Yes, in the previous verse we are told to strive for perfection in our Christian lives, but now we are being informed that the Lord is working in our lives toward the same goal. As John 15:4 tells us, unless we abide in Christ we can do nothing. True, we are to work out our salvation, but we can do so only in the energy which the Lord supplies (*cf.* 1 Peter 4:10, 11). Our spiritual maturity begins with and is thoroughly dependent upon God.

It is instructive to know that the Greek word for "work" in this verse is totally different from the one for "work" in verse 12. In verse 12 the word meant "to work out toward a goal." In verse 13, this word means "to energize." We get our "energy" from the Lord, and growth is possible only because of that energy.

What exactly does the Lord energize us to do? Two things: First, to desire His good pleasure. The words "to will" in the text are the translation of a Greek word meaning "to desire." God produces the desire to do His will in the heart of the saints as we subject ourselves to the Holy Spirit's ministry. Scripture teaches that even our desire to please God is energized by Him. That does not mean that we cannot stifle that desire, but it does mean that we are not responsible to produce the motivation to live for God—that's His job. And He will produce this desire in our lives as we trust and abide in Him.

Second, the Lord energizes us to act according to His good pleasure. Because our desires will ultimately direct our lives, God does not give us the desire to do His will without also supplying the power to do it. Our Lord has supplied all that we need to grow up in Him. Now we must take what is supplied and grow.

Maturity is the result of human response to the enablement of God. It is initiated by God and requires a radical dependence upon the grace and power of the Spirit as we work out our salvation.

This manual is designed to aid the children of God in the process of working out their salvation through the power and energy that God supplies. By the Lord's grace, may it accomplish this purpose in your life.

Lesson #1

New Life

At the moment of your conversion, when you confessed by faith alone Jesus Christ as your Savior and Lord, you were brought into a wonderful new life and relationship with God. Many things happened when you trusted Jesus Christ for forgiveness of sin. In this first lesson we explore some of those things, beginning with examining what the Bible says happened to you at the moment of conversion. Then we will see what it has to say about assurance of salvation.

I. YOUR ETERNAL SALVATION

At the moment of salvation, you were:

Redeemed (1 Peter 1:18–19). This is the act of God whereby He paid the price of your sins. He purchased sinners through the death of Christ, and as a result forgives our sin (Colossians 1:14). But not only have we been forgiven, we have been justified.

Justified. This is a legal term meaning "declare righteous" (Romans 3:24; 5:1). This means that Jesus Christ took our sins and placed them on His account (1 Peter 2:24), and in return credited us with His righteousness (Philippians 3:9; 2 Corinthians 5:21).

Given peace with God (Romans 5:1). The result of justification is peace with God (Ephesians 2:17). Your conscience is cleared and the guilt is lifted because you know you have been reconciled to God (that is, you were once separated from God but the differences are settled [Romans 5:8 10]).

Given an inheritance (1 Peter 1:4). You are now complete in Christ; nothing more needs to be added to give you eternal life (Colossians 2:9 10).

You possess every spiritual blessing (Ephesians 1:3). Every gift the Holy Spirit gives, you have been given.

You have assurance of eternal life (1 Peter 1:4).

Given a new position. You are now a member of a holy and royal priesthood (1 Peter 2:5, 9); a citizen of heaven (Philippians 3:20); a member in the family of God by birth (John 3:5) and by adoption (Galatians 4:5).

Given new possibilities. Because you are now in the family of God, many wonderful things are possible for you.

- You can begin to understand in a fuller way God's Word (1 Corinthians 2:12, 14).

- You can obtain strength to apply the Word to change selfish habit patterns (1 Corinthians 10:13; Philippians 4:13).

- You can experience joy in trials (James 1:2–4; Romans 8:28–29).

- You can have fellowship with other believers in the church of Christ (1 John 1:7–9).

- You are now part of the body of Christ (Ephesians 4:16; 1 Corinthians 12:12–13).

II. YOUR ASSURANCE OF ETERNAL SALVATION

How do you know that you really have eternal life? Let us see what Scripture says:

Read 1 John 5:11, 12. *God says, The witness is this, that God has given us* _____*, and this life is in* _____
_____.

Note: The witness is <u>not</u> based on <u>feelings</u>, but on God's Word.

Circle the correct word taken from 1 John 5:12: *These things have I written to you… that you may* (think) (feel) (wish) (suppose) (hope) (know) *that you have eternal life.*

Read 1 Peter 1:3–5. What are three descriptions of your inheritance, which is reserved in heaven?

_____

_____

_____

What is the significance of the inheritance being reserved in Heaven? (v. 5)

_____

How confident in His keeping power may you be (2 Timothy 1:12)? According to Philippians 1:6, why can we have this confidence?

_____

Note: Our assurance of eternal life is beneficial in many ways, but its main purpose is to enable us to live and grow in the likeness of Christ (Romans 8:28–29a).

Why can believers be confident they cannot lose their salvation? (John 10:27–28)

_____

Your eternal salvation is guaranteed by:

The Savior's _____ (John 5:24).

The Savior's _____ (John 10:28 30).

The Savior's _____
(Romans 8:35, 37–39).

The Savior's _____
(Ephesians 1:13; 4:30).

The Savior's _____ (2 Timothy 1:12; Jude 24)

If you are not in Christ, you have eternal death (Revelation 20:14–15). If you have received Christ, you have eternal life (1 John 5:13).

According to John 5:24, the believer has already passed from _____ to _____.

What are some evidences of eternal life?

1 John 5:13

_____

1 John 3:14

_____

1 John 2:5

_____

At times you may be tempted to doubt your salvation because you don't feel saved. God wants you to avoid the tragic mistake of **basing your life on your feelings**. He wants you to begin basing your life on that which can never fail: the eternal Word of God! **Faith is not based on the five senses, but faith is always acting on God's promises** (Hebrews 11:1–6; Romans 4:20–21).

Lesson #2

Basic Understandings

A group of tourists visiting a picturesque village walked by an old man sitting beside a fence. In a rather patronizing way, one tourist asked, "Were any great men born in this village?" The old man replied, "Nope, only babies."

A patronizing question brought a profound answer. There are no instant heroes, whether in this world or in the kingdom of God. No great Christians have ever been born. Maturity takes time, effort, and the power of God in our lives. The question we must address is: **How do believers grow in righteousness?**

In *Godliness Through Discipline*, Jay Adams states: "There are only two kinds of life: the feeling-motivated life of sin oriented toward self, and the commandment-motivated life of holiness oriented toward godliness." You need to understand several basic things in order to grow in godliness.

I. YOU MUST UNDERSTAND YOUR NEW POSITION IN CHRIST

According to Ephesians 2:1–3, what are 5 descriptions of your life before you became a Christian?

_____

_____

_____

_____

_____

According to Ephesians 2:4–6, what are 3 descriptions of your life now as a believer?

_____

_____

_____

How should we view ourselves as Christians?

2 Corinthians 5:17

_____

Romans 6:11

_____

Romans chapter 6 teaches that we are no longer under the power of sin; nevertheless, sinless perfection cannot be obtained in this life. The reason is that we still live in the "flesh" or the "body" that houses the principle of sin (Romans 6:12–7:25). While our inward nature has been changed and is dead to sin, our body is still alive to sin until it is changed at the resurrection (1 Corinthians 15:42–44). Because the believer still battles with sin, it is important that we understand the nature of temptation.

II. YOU MUST UNDERSTAND THE NATURE OF TEMPTATION

Read the following passages and note the three sources of temptation.

James 1:13–14

_____

1 John 2:15–16

_____

1 Peter 5:8; 2 Corinthians 11:13–14

_____

How did Jesus overcome temptation? (Matthew 4:2–11)

_____

_____

We have this same resource for overcoming temptation.

In 2 Timothy 3:16–17, note four ways in which God's Word is useful for overcoming sinful habits:

_____

_____

_____

_____

What is God's promise in 1 Corinthians 10:13? (Write this verse out.)

_____

_____

_____

_____

What excuses have you made for sin?

_____

What is your avenue of escape in a current trial?

_____

If this promise is true, why do you sin at times?

_____

What resources for victory are at your disposal?

_____

III. YOU MUST UNDERSTAND GOD'S <u>PURPOSES</u> FOR THE BELIEVER IN THIS LIFE

Although there are many purposes for the believer, there are three primary ones, and even these overlap.

What is God's purpose for the believer in Romans 8:28–29?

_____

_____

What is God's purpose for the believer in 2 Corinthians 5:9?

_____

_____

What is God's purpose for the believer in 1 Corinthians 10:31?

_____

_____

It is important that we understand God's purposes for our lives; otherwise, our priorities in life will be wrong and we will misinterpret what God is attempting to accomplish in our lives. According to Matthew 6:33, our priorities should be what?

_____

_____

IV. YOU MUST UNDERSTAND THAT GOD <u>EXPECTS</u> OBEDIENCE

What does God desire of us in Romans 12:1–2?

_____

_____

According to Romans 6:12–13, what must we do if we are to be **obedient** to God?

_____

In order to grow in Christ, what three things does Ephesians 4:22–24 tell us to do?

_____

_____

_____

The "put-off, put-on" dynamic is found consistently throughout the Bible. Growth will not take place by simply putting off sinful behavior. For example, if you decide to stop a bad habit but do nothing to replace that habit, growth will not take place and you will soon return to your former way of living. You must **replace** sinful behavior with godly patterns of living.

List side-by-side several sinful habits and what those habits should be replaced with according to Ephesians 4:25–32.

PUT OFF	PUT ON

How can we obtain the **power and the desire** to obey God's Word?

Galatians 5:16

_____

John 15:7, 8

_____

Philippians 4:12–13

_____

What will be the result of living such a life? (Galatians 5:22–23)

_____

_____

V. CONCLUSION

God does not expect us to be perfect (Philippians 3:12), He expects us to be **growing** (Philippians 3:14).

This lesson highlights some of the biblical principles that you must understand if you are to grow in godliness; however, growth will also require discipline. There will be little growth in your Christian life unless you discipline yourself to study the Scriptures, spend time in prayer, enjoy quality fellowship, worship God, and learn how to become dependent upon the Holy Spirit. In subsequent lessons, we will study these basic disciplines.

Lesson #3

God's Word

When a person becomes a child of God, he or she now has the Holy Spirit living within him or her. The Holy Spirit will enable that person to have the power to live the Christian life. Nevertheless, God's Spirit does not act independently of God's Word. In order to overcome sinful habits, grow in godliness, and obtain guidance for everyday living, we must read and act upon God's Word in faith. Whenever God requires anything of His children, He always provides instruction and power to meet those requirements through His Holy Word.

I. THE IMPORTANCE OF GOD'S WORD

We must understand what the Bible is and what it can do in our lives.

Approximately 39 men of God wrote the Scriptures under special inspiration over a period of 1,500 years. Who inspired these men? (2 Timothy 3:16)

_____

The word *inspired* means "God-breathed." Although God used men as His instruments, who is the primary author of the Scriptures? (2 Peter 1:19–21)

_____

Read 2 Timothy 3:15–17.

What is the most important thing the Scriptures teach us? (v. 15)

_____

Because the Scriptures are God-breathed, they are profitable for _____, for _____, for _____, and for _____ (v. 16).

What does God's Word **enable** us to do? (v. 17)

_____

From the following verses, note the attitudes we should have toward the Word of God.

Psalm 119:35

_____

Psalm 119:42

_____

Psalm 119:62

_____

Psalm 119:117

_____

Psalm 119:164

_____

Psalm 119:167

_____

We must understand the importance of not only knowing but also **obeying** God's Word.

What will prove our love for Christ? (John 14:15, 21, 23)

_____

Read John 15:4–10 and list three requirements that are necessary for bringing forth fruit.

_____

_____

_____

According to Galatians 5:22, 23, what is the "fruit" of the Spirit?

_____

_____

_____

What is commanded in James 1:22?

_____

_____

We are responsible for growing in our Christian life, but who enables us to do so, according to Philippians 2:12–13?

_____

II. HOW TO USE GOD'S WORD

There are several ways in which we can develop a deeper understanding of God's Word and, through the application of Scripture, develop lives that glorify and please God. For example:

Listen to the Word of God as it is being taught

Read Ephesians 4:11–16. What obligation does God give to pastor-teachers and evangelists today?

_____

Timothy was a pastor in the early church. What instructions does Paul give to him in 2 Timothy 4:1–2?

Read and study God's Word

By reading God's Word we can obtain a good knowledge of the Bible. A few minutes of reading each day can greatly improve our understanding of the Scriptures. You may want to make it your goal to read through the Bible in a year. In order to do so, you would have to read three chapters a day and five on Sunday.

After we have an understanding of the overview of the Bible, we need to begin a more detailed study of God's Word. Note the content of the following verses:

Hebrews 5:12–14

---

1 Peter 2:2, 3

---

2 Timothy 2:15

We must study in order to "handle accurately" the Word of God (2 Timothy 2:15). In our study, we should apply some basic principles of interpretation:

We must interpret the Bible as we would any other piece of literature. This approach is known as "normal" interpretation. We do not try to read into, allegorize, spiritualize, or explain away what we read. Rather, we take the words of Scripture at face value, trusting that God is communicating what He wants to communicate.

Keep Scripture in its context. The words surrounding a passage will almost always throw much light upon its meaning.

Remember that Scripture interprets Scripture. The Bible does not contradict itself; therefore, an interpretation of a passage must agree with the teachings of the rest of the Word of God. When a passage is difficult to understand, a basic rule is that obscure passages must give way to clear passages.

The Bible has only one meaning in one passage. A passage does not mean one thing to one person and another thing to someone else. The question is not "What does this passage mean to me?" but "What does God intend for it to mean?" It is the purpose of Bible study to discern this latter meaning. The interpretation of a text of Scripture does not change, and it is timeless.

Meditate on and apply God's Word

Meditation is the careful contemplation and application of God's Word with the goal of conforming us to Christlikeness. We can meditate on the Scriptures by memorizing (Psalm 119:9, 11), by praying over what we have read, or by carefully and quietly considering its impact. Whatever method we use, the ultimate purpose is to apply God's truth to our lives.

What does God promise if we delight in His commandments? (Psalm 1:1–3)

_____

What is the commandment in Colossians 3:16?

_____

_____

What four actions are mentioned in Psalm 119:15–16?

_____

_____

_____

_____

What are some principles found in James 1:22–25?

_____

Use this chart as a guide for Bible study, meditation, and application of the Word.

Passage being studied: James 1:22 25

OBSERVATION	INTERPRETATION	APPLICATION

As we study God's Word, we should do so in order to discover and apply truth to our lives for God's glory. We should not be looking for an emotional lift, or some great experience that will immediately change our lives. The Word of God is not a magic wand that, when read, will erase all of our problems; rather, it is God's instructions given to us to teach us how to live life. If we go to the Bible for a "warm fuzzy" or "a pick me up," we will grow weary of reading the Scriptures when these things don't happen consistently. But when we go to the Word to learn how to live life God's way, we are coming to a well that never runs dry.

Lesson #4

Prayer

When it comes to prayer, many of us can identify with Thomas Edison's statement: "We don't know the millionth part of one percent about anything. We don't know what water is. We don't know what light is. We don't know what heat is. We have a lot of hypotheses about these things, but that is all. But we do not let our ignorance about these things deprive us of their use."

There is much about prayer that we do not understand and will not understand in this life; however, we must not allow this to rob us of the blessing and privilege of prayer. It is true that to some extent prayer will remain a mystery to us, yet at the same time, Scripture gives us much information on this subject.

I. ASPECTS OF PRAYER

God speaks to us through His Word; we speak to Him in prayer. Prayer is simply a conversation with God; nevertheless, even the disciples felt so inadequate in this area that they asked Jesus to teach them how to pray (Matthew 11:1). There are several features of prayer:

Praise/Worship

Jesus taught His disciples to begin prayers with, "Our Father, who art in Heaven, hallowed be Thy Name" (Matthew 6:9). As we enter into prayer, we should begin with worship.

The best way to learn how to praise God is by reading the Psalms. The church has long recognized that the Psalms were given to us partially to teach us how to pray.

The following Psalms are especially helpful in this way: 8, 19, 24, 29, 33, 47, 65, 77, 93, 95, 96, 97, 99, 104, 111, 113, 114, 115, 139, 147, 150, and 158. As you begin your prayer time, you may want to pray one of these psalms to God.

Another helpful thing to do is read books on the attributes of God. For example: *The Knowledge of the Holy* by Tozer, *The God You Can Know* by DeHaan, *The Attributes of God* by A.W. Pink, and *Knowing God* by Packer. The really hardy reader might want to wade through *The Existence and Attributes of God* by Charnock.

Thanksgiving

Read 1 Thessalonians 5:18. What should we be thankful for?

_____

What are some specific things for which you can thank God?

_____

Confession

What are we to confess?

_____

Confession means to be in agreement with God about the heinous nature of our sin (1 John 1:9).

How does David see his sin in Psalm 139:23–24?

_____

_____

Requests

Rather than being anxious, what does Philippians 4:6–7 tell us to do?

_____

II. HINDRANCES TO PRAYER

Sin

Psalm 68:18 tells us the Lord will not hear us if there is what in our hearts?

_____

_____

Husbands are told of one thing that will hinder their prayers in 1 Peter 3:7; what is it?

_____

Wrong motives

What is one wrong motive for prayer as described in James 4:3?

_____

_____

By contrast, what kind of motives does Jesus model in Matthew 26:39, 42?

_____

_____

Lack of faith

What does James 1:6 7 say about faith in prayer?

_____

_____

Wrong priorities

What should be our attitude toward prayer?
(1 Thessalonians 5:17)

_____

_____

How does Matthew 6:33 help us here?

_____

_____

Sleepiness: Walk or sit in such a way that sleep is not easy.

Interruptions: Have a special time and place for prayer every day. Try to choose a place where you will encounter as few people as possible, when phone calls and texts will be at a minimum, and where the noise level will be low. Ask your family to help you in your desire to meet with God.

Wandering thoughts: Pray aloud—this will aid in your concentration. Keep paper and pen handy to jot down things that come to mind that may cause you to lose your train of thought (e.g., a phone call that you will need to make or things you must do today).

III. PUBLIC PRAYER

Public prayer is an important part of our lives. Our prayers should be humble, not given to impress others.

Men are to be leaders in public prayers in the church
(1 Timothy 2:8).

Family prayer is vital, as Christ should be central in our families.

IV. CONCLUSION

Consider the following quotes on prayer:

"I have lived to thank God that all my prayers have not been answered." —Jean Ingelow

"When God grants our prayers, it is because He loves us. When He does not, it is also because He loves us." —O. Hallesby

Now unto Him who is able to do exceeding abundantly beyond all that we ask or think, according to the power that works within us, to Him be the glory. (Ephesians 3:20–21)

Lesson #5

Dealing With Sin

God's plan is for the believer to grow in the likeness of Christ. Growth, not perfection, is His expectation. As long as we are in these bodies, we will have to deal with sinful thought patterns, actions, and habits; therefore, it is essential to our progression that we know the means God has provided for us to clear our conscience, to stay in proper fellowship with Him, and to continue to mature spiritually.

Our old way of handling sin must change. As unsaved people, we handled sin the way Adam and Eve did: we hide, we run, we shift blame, we cover over sin so that God and others cannot see it. We must put off this old pattern and put on God's way of dealing with sin.

I. THE SERIOUSNESS OF SIN

List the results of sin as found in the following passages:

Psalm 32:3–4

_____

Psalm 38:2–10

_____

1 John 2:11

_____

28

James 4:1–3 (note what we become when sin controls us)

_____

_____

What did David expect to happen after he confessed his sin to God? (Psalm 51:12–13)

_____

II. DEALING WITH SIN GOD'S WAY

When we sin, we can handle it the way Adam and Eve did, or we can handle it as the Scriptures teach. There are several elements involved in dealing with sin God's way:

Confession

According to 1 John 1:9, what is the believer to do when the light of God's Word shows him that he has sinned?

_____

The word "confess" means "to say the same thing" or "to agree with God about my sin." What did David call it in Psalm 51:1–4?

_____

Repentance

Not all sorrow over sin accomplishes God's purposes. What does 2 Corinthians 7:10 have to say about this?

_____

Why would a person be sorry about her sins but not genuinely repentant?

_____

The word repent simply means "to change direction" or to "turn around and go the opposite way." So, repentance is a **change of mind** that leads to a change of **action** concerning sin, self, and God.

Change

What relationship does **repentance** have to our **actions** in the following passages?

Matthew 3:8

_____

Acts 26:20

_____

According to Ephesians 4:22–24, what has to happen for this change to take place?

_____

The Gospel

The gospel is the means by which God deals with our sin. Through the cross, on which Christ died in our place, forgiveness is now possible.

III. DEALING WITH SIN AGAINST PEOPLE

How are we to handle it when we have sinned not only against God, but against another person as well? Scripture teaches that we are to confess and repent of our sin to God, and that we must also do the following with the one we sinned against.

Repent

If we are to receive forgiveness from another, what must we do? (Luke 17:3)

_____

When should we do this? (Matthew 5:22, 23)

_____

Restitution

This should be a natural reaction on the part of any truly repentant believer. Note Zacchaeus' attitude in Luke 19:8:

_____

What does Philemon 18 and 19 say?

_____

_____

What about when we cannot resolve an issue or when the offended person refuses to forgive? (Romans 12:18–19)

_____

Lesson #6

Baptism and the Lord's Supper

I. BAPTISM

In the Great Commission (Matthew 28:19–20), Jesus commanded His disciples to go and make disciples by baptizing and teaching them to obey His commandments.

Who *should be baptized?*

According to Matthew 28:19–20, who is to be baptized?

Who did the Apostles baptize?

Acts 8:35–38

Acts 16:30–34

There is no indication in the New Testament that infants were ever baptized.

Why *should a believer be baptized?*

Obedience to God's Word. Christ commanded baptism (Matthew 28:19), and it was practiced in the New Testament church (Acts 2:41).

Identification with Jesus Christ. In the clothing industry of that day, a piece of cloth would be immersed or dipped or "baptized" into a vat of dye, thus "identifying with" the color of that dye. When we are baptized, we are identifying with Christ in His death, burial, and resurrection. It is a testimony to the world and before God that we have died to sin and have risen with Christ to newness of life (read Romans 6:13–16).

How should a believer be baptized?

The Greek word for "baptize" means to "dip or immerse." The word was never translated into English in our Bibles but rather transliterated because of fear of the established church. When the King James Version was written, the church was already practicing unbiblical modes of baptism; therefore, the translators feared that if they used the word "immerse," their translation would be rejected. Of course, our modern versions have done the same thing for the same reason.

Baptism also symbolizes the Holy Spirit's work in cleansing us and immersing us into the body of Christ (1 Corinthians 12:13).

Which mode of baptism fits the thought of the following passages: sprinkling, pouring, or immersion? John 3:23; Acts 8:36–39; Colossians 2:12

_____

_____

The mode of baptism is to be immersion, as proven by the meaning of the word, the symbolism behind the act, and the practice of the early church.

When should a believer be baptized?

After reading all the preceding verses, at what point should the believer be baptized? (See Acts 8:36–38.)

_____

II. THE LORD'S SUPPER

Purpose

What is the purpose of the Lord's Supper, sometimes called Communion, the Table of the Lord, or the Eucharist? What did Jesus do? Why did He do it? What does it symbolize? These are important questions. To get a handle on them, we need to turn to Luke 22 and start with the initial giving of the Supper at the Passover meal that Jesus shared with His disciples in the upper room.

According to Luke 22:17–20, what two elements are partaken of at the Lord's Table?

_____

As Jesus takes the cup, He gives thanks and instructs the apostles to share the cup with each other. In turn, He does the same with the bread. As we come to the Table, we come to celebrate our commonality in Christ. When we come to the Table, we do not come together merely as individuals: we come as a body, and we partake as one body of the common cup.

What does Jesus say the cup symbolizes?

_____

What does Jesus say the bread symbolizes?

_____

The key phrase in the account is "given for you," meaning that Christ was giving Himself for us as our sacrificial offering. The Lord died for us. He gave Himself as a substitutionary offering. He died in our place. Had He not done so, we could not be saved, for it would be necessary for us to pay for our own sins—something impossible for us to do. It was necessary for Christ to die as our substitutionary atonement.

The gospel message is that Jesus Christ died in our place and shed His blood for us. This is the pure and simple gospel. The Supper commemorates that simple gospel message. It is a constant reminder of our sinful condition and what Christ did to remedy our condition.

In remembrance

In 1 Corinthians 11:25, Paul, in reference to the Communion, says that Jesus told us to participate for what reason?

_____

The Table emphasizes the remembrance of what Christ has done for us. It is a time of memorial. As a time of remembrance of what He has done for us, the Supper becomes of utmost importance in the life of the believer. It functions as a reminder of the great sacrifice of Christ on our behalf, and as we participate, it becomes perhaps the highest and holiest moment of our worship of Christ.

The Supper in practice

If you visit a variety of local churches of various denominations, you will find that the Table is practiced in many different ways. In some congregations, believers remain seated while the elements are brought to them. In many assemblies, believers come forward to receive the elements from the leaders, or serve themselves, and then return to their seats. Also, the Supper is observed at various frequencies by different churches and traditions. Some churches practice the Lord's Supper every Sunday morning, while others do so during an evening service. Others offer Communion once per month, or once per quarter. I even have heard of one tradition in which the Lord's Supper is an annual event—but the main spiritual event of the year. The believers come together for a whole weekend to examine their lives, confess their sins, and celebrate the Lord's Supper. The manner and frequency of the Table is not mandated in Scripture and thus is not a matter of essential doctrine which should be divisive among followers of Christ.

Lesson #7

The Church

I. DEFINING THE CHURCH

God's care for you does not stop after you are saved. Part of His plan for your growth and conformity to Christ's image is accomplished through the functions of the local church. Being a vital part of a scriptural, local New Testament church is God's intended plan for every believer, and we are admonished not to forsake the assembling of ourselves together (Hebrews 10:25).

Nowhere in the New Testament is there a believer who does not become involved in a local assembly. According to the pastoral epistles of Timothy and Titus, these assemblies were to be organized according to the given New Testament pattern and instruction. We need to understand the importance of what God says regarding New Testament churches.

The term church is derived from the Greek word "ecclesia," which means "called-out ones" (Acts 15:14).

The universal church

The church in this sense consists of the entire body of believers from the day of Pentecost (Acts 2) until the Rapture (1 Thessalonians 4:16 17). Every person who is saved is a part of this body.

As believers, each of us are members of what?
(1 Corinthians 12:12–13)

_____

The local church

The primary usage of the term church in the New Testament refers to local churches. Ninety out of 111 times the word is used in this way. A true church is established according to the design found in the New Testament.

The local church is a body of baptized believers convening together to carry out the commission given by its Head, Jesus Christ (Matthew 28:19–20).

The Bible never refers to a local church as being part of any larger earthly organization. Although denominations consisting of many churches exist, the New Testament speaks of individual local churches such as "the seven churches which are in Asia..." (Revelation 1:4, 11, 20). God's plan for this age involves His work being carried on through local, self-governing, self-supporting, and self-propagating churches.

Scriptural characteristics of the local church

Jesus Christ is its foundation (1 Corinthians 3:11).

Jesus Christ is its head. What do we learn about Christ's headship over the church in Ephesians 5:23?

_____

_____

The Scriptures teach several purposes of the local church:

To glorify God.

In what ways can we glorify God? (1 Peter 2:9–12)

_____

_____

To evangelize (Matthew 28:19–20).

To edify and equip (Ephesians 4:11–16).

What are the purposes of the church as found here?
(Ephesians 4:11–12)

_____

_____

What will this prevent? (v. 14)

_____

What is our goal? (vv. 15–16)

_____

What is needed to accomplish this goal? (2 Timothy 3:15–17)

_____

_____

What should we be trying to do when we come together?
(Hebrews 10:24, 25)

_____

To encourage one another (Hebrews 10:24–25)

_____

To serve one another (1 Corinthians 12:7)

_____

Additional characteristics of the church

It has membership (Acts 2:41, 47).

It transacts business.

Matthias chosen (Acts 1).

Deacons chosen (Acts 6).

Missionaries sent (Acts 11:22; 13:1–4).

Missionaries supported (1 Corinthians 16:2–3).

Practices discipline with the goal of restoring believers (2 Corinthians 5). In this process members can be excluded or restored (2 Corinthians 2:6–8).

It is given commissions, ordinances, and Pastoral Epistles for order (lesson 8 covers these).

II. ORGANIZATION OF THE LOCAL CHURCH

Head

The Head of the Church (local and universal) is Jesus Christ (Ephesians 5:22–24).

In John 16:12 14, we learn that our Lord, as Head of the church, is currently directing the church's activities through the leadership of the _____.

Read Ephesians 6:17. The Holy Spirit uses the sword of the Spirit, which is the _____
_____, to guide His church.

Officers

Elders

Throughout the New Testament we find several terms used for the same office. These include *shepherd, overseer, bishop,* and *pastor.* These are not separate offices but different terms or titles that help describe the same office.

39

Elder means (Titus 1:5)

_____

Overseer means (1 Timothy 3:2)

_____

Shepherd means (1 Peter 5:1–2)

_____

Pastor-teacher means (Ephesians 4:11)

_____

What are the qualifications for an elder? (1 Timothy 3:1–7)

_____

_____

_____

_____

What are the responsibilities of an elder?

Acts 20:28, 31

_____

1 Peter 5:1–3

_____

Hebrews 13:17

_____

Ephesians 4:11–16

_____

1 Timothy 5:17 (note that not all elders teach)

Deacons

Deacon means "servant." In Acts 6:1–7 we have the appointing of what many believe to be the first deacons of the church. What was their responsibility?

Other officers

The local church is free under the guidance of the Word of God to choose other officers as needed, but no other offices are found in the New Testament with the possible exception of deaconess (1 Timothy 3:11).

III. MEMBERSHIP IN A CHURCH

What occurred after people were saved? (Acts 2:41)

Note the events that preceded membership in the local church (Acts 3:37–41):
- Conviction
- Repentance and faith
- Baptism

In Acts 2:41 we find that immediately after their salvation and baptism, believers were "added to" or became members of the local church in Jerusalem. In the New Testament we never find a believer who was not a member of a church, committed to a local body, and under the authority of the elders of that church. It is God's will that every Christian be under the preaching, teaching, care, and warmth of a local church body in order to grow spiritually.

The differences between attending and joining a local church include the following:

Commitment. When you join a church, you are making a statement of commitment. You are declaring that you will be loyal to a local body, and that you are dedicated to the needs and ministries of that congregation. This declaration could be comparable to the commitment of marriage versus merely dating.

Authority. When you join a church, you come under the authority of the leadership of that church. You are, in essence, allowing the shepherds of the church to watch over you for your spiritual good (Hebrews 13:17). Until you have joined a church, you have given no elders the authority to shepherd you (1 Peter 5:1–4).

Ministry. I Corinthians 12 speaks not to the universal church but to the local church at Corinth. A body cannot function if it is uncertain who its members are. The concept of the "body" implies the need for membership.

Discipline. Matthew 18:15–20 says that an unrepentant sinner who is a believer must be disciplined by the church. Which church? Obviously, the one of which the person is a member. Some may not join a church for just this reason; after all, who wants to be disciplined? However, we must remember that discipline is one of God's tools for our correction. Also, without this tool many problems between believers cannot be resolved.

Care. In 1 Timothy 5:3–10, Paul instructs Timothy on the care of widows in the local church at Ephesus. Here we find that the widows who met certain qualifications were to be added to a list

(v. 9) for apparent financial aid. The widows on the list obviously were members of the church at Ephesus, not of neighboring churches or society at large. The local church has a special obligation to care for its members, but it must know who its members are.

Lesson #8

The Holy Spirit

I. THE PERSONALITY AND DEITY OF THE HOLY SPIRIT

The Holy Spirit is a Person, as proven by the fact that He possesses the attributes of personality.

Intellect (1 Corinthians 2:10, 11)

Emotion (Ephesians 4:30)

Will (1 Corinthians 12:11)

The Holy Spirit is God as proven by His titles. What is He called in the following passages?

Matthew 1:20

_____

Matthew 3:16

_____

Luke 1:35

_____

His attributes. What does He possess that proves He is God?

1 Corinthians 2:11, 12

_____

Psalm 139:7

_____

Job 33:4

_____

1 John 5:7

_____

Luke 11:13

_____

His actions: What does He do that only God can do?

Genesis 1:2

_____

2 Peter 1:21

_____

John 3:6

_____

Romans 8:26

_____

II. THE CHANGING MINISTRY OF THE HOLY SPIRIT

The ministry of the Holy Spirit today is not as it was in the Old Testament nor during the transition period between the Old and New Testaments.

In the Old Testament, not all believers were indwelt and sealed by the Holy Spirit. He (the Holy Spirit) moved upon certain ones for special tasks. Read the following passages and note how God gave His people power in order to accomplish His will.

Judges 14:5–6, 19

_____

1 Samuel 16:12–14

_____

2 Chronicles 24:18–20

_____

The New Testament or church age does not begin until Acts 2 at the coming of the Holy Spirit. The book of Acts records the transitional age.

What did Jesus promise in Acts 1:4–5?

_____

_____

What was Jesus saying in John 14:16–17?

_____

_____

God delayed sending the Holy Spirit until the Day of Pentecost. According to Acts 2:4–9, what happened at this time among the Jews?

_____

In Acts 8:14–17, the Samaritans receive the gospel but do not receive the Holy Spirit until the Apostles come.

In Acts 10:44–45, the Gentiles receive the Holy Spirit.

In Acts 19:1–6, a group of Old Testament saints receive the Holy Spirit.

Today all believers receive the Holy Spirit at the moment of conversion.

What does Romans 8:9 say?

_____

III. THE MINISTRY OF THE HOLY SPIRIT

What is the Holy Spirit's relationship to the Scriptures (2 Peter 1:21; 2 Timothy 3:16–17)?

_____

What is the Holy Spirit's relationship to man, according to John 14:16–17?

_____

What ministries does the Holy Spirit perform in relationship to our salvation?

Titus 3:5

_____

1 Corinthians 6:19

_____

1 Corinthians 12:13

_____

Ephesians 1:13–14

_____

Other ministries of the Holy Spirit

Ephesians 5:18

_____

To be "filled by" means to be "controlled by."

John 16:12–15

_____

1 Corinthians 2:9–14

_____

Romans 8:26

_____

Galatians 5:22–24

_____

Acts 1:8

_____

IV. SPIRITUAL GIFTS

The Holy Spirit gives the believer spiritual gifts. These are defined as "God-given abilities for service."

When does a believer receive His gifts? (1 Corinthians 12:7, 18)

_____

Who decides what gifts a believer receives?
(1 Corinthians 12:11, 18)

_____

Why has God given different gifts? (1 Corinthians 12:24–25)

_____

Lists of the various spiritual gifts are found in 1 Corinthians 12
and in the following:
- Romans 12:6–8

- Ephesians 4:11

- 1 Peter 4:10–11

How to find your spiritual gifts
- Know the biblical gifts.

- Serve where you can. In this way you will begin to
  discover where you are fruitful.

- Get counsel from wise, mature Christians.

- Develop your gifts. One bad experience with something
  does not mean you don't have the gift.

- Knowing the exact name or title for your spiritual
  giftedness is not as important as useful service. Each
  Christian is uniquely equipped by God to minister
  for Him. The Lord bundles our personalities, talents,
  intellect, and gifts into a one-of-a-kind individual
  especially suited for His purpose and design.

Lesson #9

Getting Along with God's People

Christ told His disciples: "By this [your love for one another] shall all men know that you are my disciples" (John 13:34–35). In Ephesians 4:16, Paul describes a healthy church as one in which every member is meeting needs; as a result, the body is not only healthy but also increasing. Hebrews 10:24 commands believers to stimulate one another to love and good works. There are numerous passages in the New Testament exhorting believers to love and care for "one another."

This love and care for one another is not to cease when a Christian does wrong. In Galatians 6:1, Paul tells the believer living for God to "restore" others who are "overtaken in a fault." Scripture has much to say about this process.

I. PERSONAL EXAMINATION

As we examine ourselves, we may recognize that we have genuinely offended someone else. It is possible that someone is angry at us or even hates us, yet we have not wronged them. Such a case is not being discussed in Matthew 5:23–24. It is not always possible to be at peace with everyone (Romans 12:18). If everyone has to be pleased with us before we worship God, then neither Jesus nor the apostles would ever have worshipped.

But when we have wronged another, what are we commanded to do in Matthew 5:23–24?

_____

How long should you wait before you deal with the one you offended?

What if you "know" that the ones offended will reject you? What if you don't think that now is the right time for reconciliation?

II. HOW TO DEAL WITH SOMEONE WHO HAS SINNED AGAINST US

Note the steps taken in Matthew 18:15–17.

First, **determine if this issue is a sin issue** (read Galatians 6:1). The text is not talking about personal preferences, differences of opinion, or conviction, but of definite sin.

"Go." We do not wait for others to come to us; rather, we are to go to them. It is much easier sometimes just to ignore the person or "write them off," but love says "go" (notice the context in Matthew 18:12–14).

"Convince." To tell or show him his fault; this text uses a strong word meaning to "convict or convince." Why is it so important that we convince people of their sin rather than simply letting them go their way?

If Genesis 3:8–13 is any indication of their possible response, what reactions must we be prepared to deal with when we confront people with their sins?

According to Matthew 18:15, should people be approached in front of others?

_____

If not, then how are they to be approached?

_____

_____

What is the **goal** of the following verses?

Matthew 18:15

_____

Galatians 6:1

_____

James 5:20

_____

Small-group confrontation (Matthew 18:16)

If the previous step fails, then we do not simply walk away. We must approach the person again, this time with a small group of two or three. Why is this step necessary?

_____

*Confrontation from the church (Matthew 18:17a) and **church discipline** (Matthew 18:17b)*

What is the **goal** of church discipline? (1 Corinthians 5:5)

_____

This final step is a last resort, and no timetable is given to us as to when it must take place. If progress is being made or if the person is not going into deeper sin or influencing others in a negative way, then there is no need to rush to step 6, but it should not be ignored either.

In Matthew 18:18–19, we are told that when this final step has been taken by the church, it has already been taken in heaven. In other words, **we are to be in agreement with God**. God has recognized the person's unrepentant sin and so should we.

Such a person is to be treated as a "pagan." Given that at this stage **the goal is still to restore**, we are to continue to be friendly and kind. However, the individual is not to be recognized as a brother in Christ. If, for instance, he is a family member, you may eat with him as a family member, but not as a fellow believer (1 Corinthians 5:11). The goal is restoration, which demands that we take God's side and do things God's way. God calls believers who are in sin to repent…so should we.

III. THE SUBJECT OF FORGIVENESS

Forgiveness is not a feeling; it is a promise.

When we forgive, we promise no longer to hold a wrong against someone. We are in essence promising never to bring up the offense to the offender, to others, or to ourselves again.

According to Luke 17:3–4, who are we to forgive?

Why is it not possible to fully forgive an unrepentant person?

How do we know if the person is sincere in his or her repentance?

_____

_____

In Matthew 18:21–35, what does Jesus say about the person who refuses to forgive?

_____

How are we to treat a person who will not repent of wrongs done to us? (Romans 12:14, 17–21)

_____

_____

IV. CONCLUSION

Who taught this method of dealing with offenses against one another?

_____

Do you agree with Him?

_____

Do you practice what He taught?

_____

When a person comes to share a problem with you about someone else, how should you tell the sharer to handle it, according to Matthew 18:15?

_____

_____

Lesson #10

Biblical Love

There is much fuzziness about "love" in our culture today. Because it plays such an important role in our world, as well as our Christian lives and churches, it is vital that we know what Scripture has to say on the subject.

I. THE IMPORTANCE OF LOVE

What commandment did Christ give to His disciples the night before He went to the cross? (John 13:34, 35)

_____

_____

Obedience to this command would produce what results?

_____

_____

How is the love that demonstrates Christlikeness produced in our lives? (Galatians 5:22)

_____

_____

In relation to all other virtues and actions, how highly does God rate love? (1 Corinthians 13:1–3, 13)

_____

II. WHAT IS BIBLICAL LOVE?

Note the characteristics of love as found in 1 Corinthians 13:4 8a.

Do these characteristics put more emphasis on actions or feelings?

_____

If one word could be used to describe love, what would it be, according to John 3:16?

_____

Is the emphasis here on actions or feelings?

_____

Where is the emphasis in 1 John 3:17–18?

_____

Can love be taught? (1 Thessalonians 4:9; Titus 2:4)

_____

Biblically, what should we tell spouses who want to divorce because they no longer love their mates?

_____

_____

_____

To love is a command from God (Matthew 22:36–40).

Can we command our emotions?

_____

Is the emphasis here on actions or emotions?

_____

Who is the supreme example of love? (Ephesians 5:25)

The Greek word *agape*, which is translated as "love" in these passages, speaks of a self-sacrificing love. It does not have reference to emotions or feelings. Agape love may include feelings, and hopefully does, but emotions are not at the heart of such love.

Love is a command to be obeyed—
- not an option
- not an accident
- not a feeling to be generated first

III. WHO ARE WE TO LOVE?

Matthew 22:36–37

Luke 10:29–37

John 13:34–35

Titus 2:4

Ephesians 5:25

Matthew 5:44

Romans 12:14, 17–21

IV. WHAT DOES IT MEAN TO "WALK IN LOVE"?

Love God and His Word (John 14:21; 15:10; 1 John 5:3).

Put others ahead of yourself (Philippians 2:3–4;
Romans 12:20 21).

Perform loving deeds and actions as well as speak kind words
(1 John 3:18).

Be a giver (Acts 20:35; John 3:16).

Be a forgiver and one who asks forgiveness (Ephesians 4:32).

Appreciate the love given to you by Christ (Romans 8:35–39).

Overcome selfishness and its emptiness (Galatians 5:19–23).

V. WHAT WILL BE THE CONSEQUENCES IF WE DO NOT WALK IN LOVE?

Problems with others

Note that the deeds of the flesh in Galatians 5:19–21 could be summed up as selfishness.

Problems with God

What does 1 John 4:7–11 teach?

_____

_____

Problems with self

Fear (1 John 4:18)

_____

Wrong values (1 John 2:15–17)

_____

VI. WHAT ARE SOME HINDRANCES TO WALKING IN LOVE?

Separation from God

Because God is the source of love, one must be united to Him through salvation in order to walk in love (1 John 4:7–10).

Adherence to false views of love

Fads concerning love will come and go. Only God's definition and description of love are correct.

Selfishness

True love will demand much of us and may give little in return. True love means we must risk being taken advantage of and hurt. True love means living for others. All of these things run contrary to our fleshly desire to live for self.

Dependency upon self

What does John 15:5 tell us?

_____

If love is a fruit of the Spirit (Galatians 5:22), how does one get it?

_____

Lesson #11

Biblical Separation

Both the Old and New Testaments are full of warnings and instructions concerning those who claim to be believers but have fallen away from the faith and now seek to drag others with them. Today the attitude even within the church is "live and let live." It seems to bother us very little that many denominations, organizations, and individuals that claim to be followers of Christ deny vital truths such as inspiration of Scripture, salvation by faith alone, the virgin birth, the deity and/or resurrection of Christ, and so on. As long as someone claims to be a Christian, we accept them with open arms, no questions asked. But to do so implies that much of the Bible was written for nothing — that somehow God is not "really" concerned about apostates. So, it is extremely important that we understand what the Bible says about apostasy.

I. DEFINITION OF APOSTASY

Apostasy consists of an unbelieving and self-willed movement away from God (Hebrews 3:12). It indicates the serious situation of denying cardinal truths and falling away from the faith.

Of course, few apostates, either today or in biblical times, would admit that they have turned from God. Therefore, it is imperative that we never separate God from His Word. This was Satan's strategy in the Garden of Eden. He never denied the existence of God; rather, he convinced Eve that God did not mean what He said.

When a person or organization falls away from the clear teachings of the Word of God, they have fallen away from God, no matter how loudly they protest. Therefore, apostasy is the act of a professed Christian or Christian organization that rejects the fundamental truths taught in God's Word. Especially important are doctrines concerning the Godhead, deity of Christ, death and resurrection of Christ, salvation by faith, inspiration of Scripture, the return of Christ, eternal life, and other doctrines that are the very backbone of the faith. Good and godly people may differ on some secondary issues, but to deny the fundamentals is apostasy.

II. THE CHARACTERISTICS OF APOSTATES

According to 2 Timothy 3:5, will apostates appear spiritual in outward appearance?

_____

Who motivates the apostates? (1 Timothy 4:1)

_____

How are apostates described in 1 Timothy 4:2?

_____

The ultimate and final apostasy on earth will occur during the Tribulation. Read 2 Thessalonians 2:2–12. What reasons are given as to why the world will believe the Antichrist's lies?

_____

_____

What are 5 characteristics of apostates found in 2 Peter 2:10?

_____

_____

_____

What do apostates promise in 2 Peter 2:19?

What do they deliver?

Note the word-pictures found in Jude 12. Briefly summarize the description given.

Read 2 Timothy 4:1–5. Unsaved people, who have no spiritual discernment, will hail Satan's teachers (1 Corinthians 11:13–15) as great religious leaders, while the preachers of truth, God's ministers, will be despised and viewed as being uncooperative, divisive, and unloving. Satan's preachers accommodate themselves to the tastes of unregenerated hearers and are thus much more popular.

III. WHEN DOES A CHURCH BODY BECOME APOSTATE?

A body does not become apostate at the time the gospel is removed from their official creed or confession. It has occurred long before this point.

A body does not become apostate when they cease to preach the gospel. It must be remembered that apostates are liars (2 Peter 2:3). They can become masters at twisting the meaning of words so that it sounds like the gospel but is not. A good example is Robert Schuller's book, *Self-Esteem: The New Reformation*.

A body is apostate at the time:
- Its leaders deny the basic tenets of the Christian faith.

- Official periodicals and media presentations promote views contrary to the clear teachings of Scripture.

- Official schools of the body employ faculty members and/or utilize visiting speakers who teach views that are at variance with essential doctrines.

- No effort is being made by the leadership or the majority of its constituency to remove the apostates within the body.

IV. HOW SHOULD THE BELIEVER HANDLE APOSTASY?

Briefly summarize the commands given in the following verses:

Romans 16:17

_____

2 Corinthians 6:14–18

_____

Galatians 1:8 9

_____

2 John 10, 11

_____

Acts 19:8–9

_____

Acts 20:28–32

Based upon these passages, should a believer stay in an apostate body and fight the apostasy?

What should a believer do?

To keep from being deceived by apostates, what are we to do?

2 Timothy 3:13–4:2

1 Timothy 4:1–6

Ephesians 4:11–16

V. CONCLUSION

Bruce Bickel writes: "Too often what passes for unity is really compromise. It is better to be divided by truth than united by error."

Yet, as David Hunt warns in *The Seduction of Christianity*, page 3, it is "in" now not to challenge one another's teachings on the basis of Scripture. He says, "There is a new push for 'unity' based not upon sound doctrine but upon the pledge not to question the biblical accuracy of one another's teachings."

MAY WE NEVER FALL INTO THIS TRAP!

Bibliography

Adams, Jay. *Godliness Through Discipline* (P&R Publishers, 1983).

Charnock, Steven. *The Existence and Attributes of God* (Baker Books, 1996).

Bickel, Bruce. *Sola Scriptura, The Protestant Position on the Bible* (Sola Deo Gloria Publications, 2000).

DeHaan, Dan. *The God You Can Know* (Moody Publishers, 2001).

Hunt, David. *Beyond Seduction: A Return to Biblical Christianity* (Harvest House, 1987).

Packer, J. I. *Knowing God* (InterVarsity Press, 1993).

Pink, A.W. *The Attributes of God* (Baker Books, 2006).

Schuller, Robert. *Self Esteem: The New Reformation* (Word Books, 1983).

Tozer, A. W. *Knowledge of the Holy* (HarperOne, 2009).

Growing Your Faith One Page at a Time

More Resources for Growing in Christ

Small Group—Sunday School—Personal Study

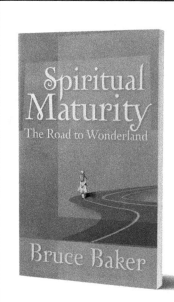

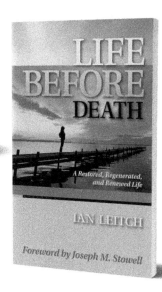

Inspirational Christian Biographies

Available at GraceAcresPress.com
or wherever books are sold.

CPSIA information can be obtained
at www.ICGtesting.com
Printed in the USA
FFHW011228261019
55767374-61632FF